CASSEROLES

Cook Books by Good Books

Phyllis Pellman Good • Rachel Thomas Pellman

Good Books

Intercourse, PA 17534
800/762-7171
www.goodbks.com

CASSEROLES

Cook Books by Good Books

We suspect that casseroles were first created in the kitchens of conscientious cooks who came up on suppertime, having no chance to make the roast or mash the potatoes.

All the eat-ers around the table agreed they worked. Those are the recipes we offer here. Sturdy and basic. Now and then a surprise. Economical. But satisfyingly filling.

Cover art and design by Cheryl A. Benner.
Design and art in body by Craig N. Heisey; Calligraphy by Gayle Smoker.
This special edition is an adaptation of *Casseroles: From Amish and Mennonite Kitchens, Pennsylvania Dutch Cookbooks.* Copyright © 1983, 1991 by Good Books, Intercourse, PA 17534.
ISBN: 1-56148-041-X. All rights reserved. Printed in the United States of America.

Contents

Crunchy Hot Chicken Casserole

3 Tbsp. butter   Makes 8 servings
¼ cup mushrooms, chopped
1 Tbsp. onion, chopped
3 Tbsp. flour
1 cup milk
1 cup celery, chopped
¾ cup mayonnaise
2 tsp. lemon juice
¾ tsp. salt
3 hard-boiled eggs, chopped
3 cups rice, cooked
2 chicken breasts, cooked and cubed
butter and Rice Krispies

1. Melt 3 Tbsp. butter. Sauté mushrooms and onion until tender. Add flour and stir until smooth. Gradually add milk and stir until thickened.
2. Combine sauce with all remaining ingredients except butter and Rice Krispies. Mix well.
3. Turn into a buttered baking dish. Sprinkle casserole with Rice Krispies. Dot with butter. Bake at 375° for 30 minutes.

Baked Chicken and Rice

½ cup plus 1 Tbsp.   Makes 6-8 servings
    butter or margarine, melted
½ cup mushrooms, chopped
¼ cup celery, chopped
½ cup plus 1 Tbsp. flour
1 Tbsp. salt
¼ tsp. pepper
4½ cups milk
1⅓ cups water
1 cup long grain rice, uncooked
dash of garlic salt
6-8 seasoned chicken parts

1. Add mushrooms and celery to melted butter in saucepan and sauté until golden. Stir in flour and seasonings. Gradually add milk and bring to the boiling point, stirring constantly until thickened. Remove from heat.
2. Blend in water. Add rice and garlic salt, mixing well.
3. Pour into large roaster or baking pan. Arrange chicken pieces on top of rice mixture.
4. Cover and bake 3 hours at 300°.

Chicken Spaghetti

1 stewing chicken	Makes 12 servings

3 Tbsp. butter or margarine
6 celery stems, chopped
2 onions, chopped
¼ cup mushrooms, chopped
3 Tbsp. flour
1 cup milk
½ lb. sharp cheese, grated
1 pint chicken stock
1 Tbsp. Worcestershire sauce
salt and pepper to taste
½ lb. spaghetti
1 small bottle stuffed olives,
    chopped or sliced
1 cup pecans, chopped

1. Cook chicken in water until tender. Remove from bones and cut in large pieces. Reserve stock.
2. Melt butter. Sauté celery, onions, and mushrooms until tender. Add flour and stir to form a smooth paste. Gradually add milk. Stir until thickened. Add cheese. Stir until melted. Add chicken stock and seasonings.
3. Cook spaghetti in water for 3 minutes.

Drain. Add to stock mixture and let stand for 1 hour. Mix in chicken and olives.
4. Pour into a 9"x 15" shallow casserole. Top with pecans. Bake at 350° for ½ hour.

Variation:
    Add 2 cups cooked peas and carrots.

Country Chicken Supper

4 oz. spaghetti,   Makes 8 servings
    uncooked
1 lb. mild cream cheese, cubed or grated
1 cup milk
½ cup mayonnaise
2 cups cooked chicken (or turkey) cubed
1½ cups peas and carrots, cooked

1. Cook spaghetti. Drain and set aside.
2. Heat cheese, milk, and mayonnaise together over low heat, stirring until sauce is smooth.
3. Add chicken, vegetables and spaghetti to sauce, mixing well. Pour into 2-quart casserole.
4. Bake at 350° for 35~40 minutes.

Chicken Broccoli Casserole

1¼ lb. fresh broccoli   Makes 10 servings
   chopped and cooked (or 2 10 oz. pkgs.),
4-6 cups cooked chicken, coarsely diced
6 Tbsp. butter or margarine
6 Tbsp. flour
2 tsp. salt
¼ tsp. pepper
3 cups milk
½ cup mayonnaise
1 tsp. lemon juice
1 cup cheddar cheese, grated
2 Tbsp. butter or margarine
½ cup bread crumbs

1. Layer broccoli on bottom of greased 9"x 13" baking dish. Layer chicken over broccoli.
2. In a saucepan melt the 6 Tbsp. butter. Stir in the flour, salt, and pepper. Gradually stir in the milk and continue stirring until the white sauce is smooth and comes to a boil. Remove from heat.
3. Combine mayonnaise and lemon juice with white sauce and pour over chicken and broccoli. Sprinkle with cheese.
4. Melt 2 Tbsp. butter. Stir in bread crumbs and sprinkle over casserole.
5. Bake at 350° for 35-40 minutes.

Chicken Macaroni Dinner

1 cup macaroni, uncooked   Makes 8 servings
1 Tbsp. butter or margarine
1 Tbsp. flour
1 tsp. salt
⅛ tsp. pepper
1 cup milk
½ cup chicken broth
1½ cups cooked chicken, diced
1 cup corn, fresh or frozen
2 Tbsp. butter, melted
½ cup bread crumbs

1. Cook macaroni. Drain and set aside.
2. Melt 1 Tbsp. butter. Stir in flour and seasonings. Gradually add milk and chicken broth. Bring to the boiling point, stirring constantly until thickened.
3. Mix together the macaroni, white sauce, chicken, and corn. Pour into a greased baking dish.
4. Stir bread crumbs into melted butter and sprinkle over casserole. Bake at 350° for 45 minutes.

Chicken Corn Pie

1 stewing chicken   Makes 6-8 servings
1 qt. corn, cooked
pastry enough for 2 double-crust pies

1. Cook chicken and remove from bones. Make a thin gravy with the chicken stock.
2. Line 2 9" pie plates with pastry. Place meat and corn in alternate layers in crust. Add gravy enough to barely cover chicken corn mixture. Cover with crust and seal edges. Bake at 425° for 20 minutes. Eat hot with remaining gravy.

Variations:
1. Delete 3 cups corn. In place of corn add cooked carrots, peas, and cubed potatoes.
2. Beef Vegetable Pie - follow above procedure but substitute 1½ lb. beef in place of chicken. Cook beef until tender. Cube and follow procedure using beef broth. Use 1 cup each peas, carrots, potatoes, and corn, cooked.

"Friday Night" Meat Pie

"When our family was growing up, I cleaned out the refrigerator every Friday evening. I gathered all the leftover vegetables and meat that had collected that week, and then cut the pork or beef or chicken into bite-sized pieces, added gravy if there was any, and stirred in all the leftover vegetables.

"If I didn't have many vegetables I diced a potato or two, added a little celery and onion, cooked them until they were soft and put them in the mixture. I also liked to add some herb seasoning.

"Then I poured it into a casserole, and dropped biscuit batter on top. I baked it, then, at 425° for 12-15 minutes.

"It's a delicious way to get rid of leftovers. Our family loved it.

"Another tip for using leftover vegetables is to keep a box in the freezing unit of the refrigerator. Then add layer upon layer of corn, peas, beans—whatever— to use in soup. The vegetables won't have a stale taste!"

Lazy Day Stew

2 lb. beef cubes   Makes 8 servings
2 cups carrots, sliced
2 cups potatoes, diced
2 medium onions, sliced
1 cup celery, chopped
1½ cups green beans
2 tsp. quick cooking tapioca
1 Tbsp. salt
½ tsp. pepper
1 8 oz. can tomato sauce
1 cup water
1 Tbsp. brown sugar

1. Place raw beef cubes (do not brown) in a single layer in a 2½ quart casserole or roast pan.
2. Add vegetables and/or any others you desire.
3. Sprinkle tapioca, salt, and pepper over top. Pour tomato sauce mixed with water over vegetables and seasonings.
4. Crumble brown sugar over all.
5. Cover tightly and do not peep! Bake at 325° for 3 hours.

Variation:
     Stew may be made in a slow cooker.

Sausage and Apple Casserole

1½ lb. link sausage   Makes 8 servings
    cut in small pieces, or
    1½ lb. bulk sausage in small balls
4 medium apples, pared and sliced
3 medium sweet potatoes, pared and
    sliced
½ tsp. salt
1 Tbsp. flour
2 Tbsp. sugar

1. Fry sausage, saving drippings.
2. Combine salt, flour, and sugar. Arrange sausage, apples, and potatoes in layers in a casserole. Sprinkle some flour mixture over each layer. Top with a layer of sausage. Sprinkle casserole with 1 Tbsp. sausage drippings. Cover tightly. Bake at 375° for 1 hour.

Six Layer Sausage Casserole

1 lb. pork sausage   Makes 6 servings
  (loose)
1½ cups raw potatoes, sliced
1 cup raw onions, sliced
1 cup raw carrots, sliced
½ cup rice, uncooked
1½ cups canned tomatoes, including juice
1 tsp. salt
⅛ tsp. pepper
2 Tbsp. sugar

1. Brown sausage in heavy skillet. Drain off excess fat.
2. Place sausage in bottom of a 2 quart casserole. Cover with layers of potatoes, onions, carrots, and rice. Add tomatoes with juice.
3. Combine salt, pepper, and sugar. Sprinkle over top. Bake, covered at 350° for 1½ hours.

Truckpatch Dinner

bacon slices
ground beef
potatoes
peas
carrots
salt and pepper to taste

1. Arrange a layer of bacon on bottom of roast pan or casserole. Add a layer of raw hamburger. Add a layer of sliced potatoes, seasoned with salt and pepper. Bake at 375° for 1 hour.
2. Remove from oven and add a layer of peas and carrots. Return to oven and bake 45-60 minutes longer.

Variation:
    Pour 1½ cups tomatoes over all before baking.

Vegetable Cheese Casserole

4 cups broccoli   Makes 6-8 servings
2 cups ham, cooked and diced
2 Tbsp. butter or margarine
2 Tbsp. flour
½ tsp. salt
1½ cups milk
¼ cup cheese, grated or cut fine
paprika
3 slices bread, buttered

1. Cook broccoli in salt water, just until tender. Put into buttered baking dish. Sprinkle ham over vegetables.
2. Melt butter. Stir in flour and salt. Gradually add milk, stirring constantly until the white sauce thickens and comes to a boiling point. Then pour over broccoli and ham.
3. Sprinkle cheese and paprika over top.
4. Cut bread in cubes and arrange on top of casserole.
5. Bake at 375° for 15-20 minutes.

Mother's Tomato Rice Meat Pie

1 lb. ground beef   Makes 12 servings
¼ cup green pepper, chopped
1 small onion, chopped
½ cup dry bread crumbs
salt and pepper to taste
2 cups tomato sauce
1⅓ cups minute rice
1 cup water
1 cup cheddar cheese, grated

1. Combine beef, pepper, onion, bread crumbs, salt, pepper, and ½ cup tomato sauce. Mix well. Pat into bottom and sides of a greased 9" square pan.
2. Combine remaining tomato sauce, rice, water, and ½ cup cheese. Spoon mixture into meat shell. Cover and bake at 350° for 25 minutes. Top with remaining cheese. Bake, uncovered 10~15 minutes longer.

Stuffed Cabbage

1 head cabbage   Makes 8-10 servings
     with large loose leaves
1 onion, minced
1 lb. ground beef
1 cup rice, cooked
1 egg, beaten
salt and pepper to taste
¼ cup tomato paste
½ cup water
1 cup cultured sour cream

1. Remove large outer leaves (8-10) from cabbage and cook in boiling salt water for 3 minutes. Drain.
2. Brown hamburger and onion together. Stir in cooked rice, egg, salt and pepper.
3. Place hamburger rice mixture on cabbage leaves. Roll up and fasten with toothpicks. Place in greased baking dish.
4. Stir together tomato paste, water, and sour cream. Then pour over cabbage rolls.
5. Cover and bake at 350° for 1 hour.

Cabbage Hamburger Bake

1 head cabbage   Makes 6-8 servings
1 lb. hamburger
3 Tbsp. butter or margarine
3 Tbsp. flour
1 tsp. salt
dash of pepper
1½ cups milk
1 tsp. parsley flakes
2 Tbsp. butter or margarine
½ cup bread crumbs

1. Slice cabbage; then steam until wilted. Spoon into greased casserole dish.
2. Brown hamburger lightly. Pour over wilted cabbage in baking dish.
3. Melt the 3 Tbsp. butter. Stir in the flour, salt, and pepper. Gradually stir in the milk and continue stirring until the white sauce is smooth and comes to a boil. Stir in the parsley flakes; then pour the sauce over the cabbage and hamburger.
4. Melt the 2 Tbsp butter. Stir in bread crumbs. Crumble over white sauce.
5. Bake at 350° for 30 minutes.

Beef, Corn, and Noodles

1 lb. hamburger,   Makes 8 servings
    browned
1 pt. corn, cooked
2 cups noodles, cooked
2 cups beef broth
1 Tbsp. butter
3 hard-boiled eggs, diced

1. Mix together the hamburger, corn, noodles, and broth. Pour into greased baking dish.
2. Dot with butter. Sprinkle egg over top.
3. Bake at 350° for 40~45 minutes.

Cheese Soufflé

2 Tbsp. butter   Makes 2 servings
3 Tbsp. flour
½ cup milk
½ cup cheese, grated
2 large or 3 small eggs, separated
½ tsp. salt

1. Melt butter. Add flour and stir to make a smooth paste. Gradually add milk. Stir until thickened. Add cheese. Stir until melted. Add egg yolks and salt.
2. Beat egg whites until stiff. Gently fold into sauce. Turn into greased casserole or soufflé dish. Bake at 325° for 25 minutes.

Baked Carrots and Apples

4 cups carrots,   Makes 7 servings
    cut in ½" pieces
3 cups apples, peeled, cored, and sliced
¼ cup honey
2 Tbsp. butter or margarine
paprika

1. Steam carrots until tender. Drain. Stir in apples and honey.
2. Turn into buttered casserole. Dot with butter. Cover and bake at 350° for 50 minutes.
3. Stir. Sprinkle with paprika. Bake, uncovered, an additional 10 minutes.

Carrot Casserole

½ cup butter   Makes 12-16 servings
1 small onion, chopped
¼ cup flour
1 tsp. salt
¼ tsp. pepper
½ tsp. dry mustard
¼ tsp. celery salt
2 cups milk
½ lb. cheese, sliced
12 large carrots, thinly sliced, cooked
buttered bread crumbs

1. Melt butter. Add onion, flour, and seasonings and stir until smooth. Gradually add milk. Stir over medium heat until thickened.
2. Arrange half of carrots in bottom of a 2½ qt. casserole. Add cheese slices. Top with remaining carrots. Pour sauce over all. Top with buttered bread crumbs. Bake at 375° for 30 minutes.

Scalloped Potatoes

6 medium potatoes   Makes 12 servings
    cooked in jackets
½ cup butter
1 tsp. parsley flakes
¼ cup onion, chopped
1 tsp. dry or prepared mustard
¼ tsp. pepper
1 tsp. salt
¼ cup milk
¼ cup cheese, grated

1.   Dice potatoes and place in greased casserole.
2.   Melt butter. Add other ingredients and cook until cheese is melted. Pour sauce over potatoes and bake at 350° for 45 minutes.

Variation:
    Omit cheese. Add 1 cup sour cream plus 1 lb. cooked, diced ham.

23

Green Beans and Potato Casserole

1½ cups cooked green   Makes 6 servings
    beans
1 cup potatoes, cooked and diced
½ cup celery, diced
4 slices bacon
1 small onion, chopped
1½ Tbsp. flour
1 cup undiluted evaporated milk
1 cup cheese, shredded
⅓ cup cracker crumbs

1. Combine beans, potatoes, and celery. Place in greased 1 quart casserole.
2. Fry bacon until crisp. Drain, saving 1 Tbsp. drippings. Crumble bacon and set aside. Sauté onion in drippings.
3. Add flour and stir to a smooth paste. Slowly add milk. Cook, stirring constantly until thickened. Add cheese. Stir until melted. Pour over vegetables in casserole and stir well.
4. Sprinkle with cracker crumbs. Add crumbled bacon on top. Bake at 350° for 30 minutes.

Zucchini Casserole

1 lb. ground   Makes 6-8 servings
    beef, browned
1½ lb. zucchini, cooked and sliced
1½ cups potatoes, cooked and cubed
½ cup cheddar cheese, shredded
salt and pepper to taste
3 Tbsp. butter
1 Tbsp. onion, minced
¼ cup mushrooms, chopped
3 Tbsp. flour
1¼ cups milk
1 cup soft bread crumbs mixed with
    2 Tbsp. melted butter

1. In buttered casserole arrange layers of beef, zucchini, potatoes, and cheese. Season to taste.
2. Melt butter. Sauté onion and mushrooms until tender. Add flour. Stir until smooth. Gradually add milk and stir until thickened. Pour sauce over layered ingredients in casserole. Top with crumbs. Bake at 350° for 1 hour.

Zucchini Scallop

2 cups zucchini, cooked   Makes 10 servings
2 cups saltine crackers, crumbled
2 Tbsp. onion, minced
1 cup cheese, cubed
1 cup milk
1 egg, beaten
2 Tbsp. butter, melted
pepper

1. Layer zucchini, crackers, onion, and cheese in a 2 qt. greased casserole. Combine milk and egg. Pour over zucchini mixture. Pour butter over all. Sprinkle with pepper.
2. Bake at 350° for 45 minutes.

Tuna Noodle Casserole

1 8 oz. pkg. noodles   Makes 24 servings
8 Tbsp. butter
5 Tbsp. flour
2½ cups milk
1 8 oz. pkg. cream cheese
1 large can tuna
salt and pepper to taste
6 oz. mild cheese, sliced
1½ cups soft bread crumbs

1. Cook noodles in water until tender. Drain and set aside.
2. Melt 5 Tbsp. of the butter. Add flour and stir to form a smooth paste. Gradually add milk and stir until thickened. Add cream cheese and tuna. Stir until cheese is melted. Add seasonings.
3. In greased casserole, layer noodles, sauce, and sliced cheese alternately.
4. Melt remaining butter. Stir in bread crumbs. Sprinkle buttered crumbs over top of casserole. Bake at 350° for 30 minutes.

Variations:
1. Use salmon in place of tuna.
2. Add 1 cup peas and 2 chopped eggs.

Easy Tuna Fondue

5 slices bread Makes 10-12 servings
½ cup cheese
1 12 oz. can tuna
2 cups milk
3 eggs, slightly beaten
½ tsp. onion, grated
paprika or parsley flakes

1. Cut bread in ½" cubes. Spread half in bottom of greased 2 qt. casserole. Sprinkle with half of cheese. Add tuna. Cover with remaining bread and cheese.
2. Combine milk, eggs, salt, and onion. Pour over mixture. Sprinkle top with paprika or parsley. Bake at 325° for 50 minutes.

Egg Strata

waffles   Makes 6-8 servings
1 lb. ham,
    cooked and ground
½ lb. cheddar cheese, grated
2 Tbsp. butter
6 eggs
3 cups milk
½ tsp. salt
¼ tsp. pepper

1. Place a single layer of waffles in bottom of a 9"x13" baking dish. Cover with ground ham. Sprinkle half of the cheese over ham. Cover with a second layer of waffles and the remaining cheese. Dot with butter.
2. Combine eggs, milk, and seasonings. Pour over waffles. Refrigerate 4 hours or overnight. Bake at 350° for 40 minutes. Remove from oven and allow to stand 10 or 15 minutes before serving.

Macaroni and Cheese

1½ cups milk, scalded

Makes 6-8 servings

2 cups soft bread crumbs or cubes (whole wheat or white)

¼ cup butter or margarine, melted

1 Tbsp. onion, chopped

1½ cups mild cheese, grated or cubed

½ tsp. salt

3 eggs, separated

1½ cups macaroni, cooked

paprika

1. Pour scalded milk over bread crumbs. Stir in butter, onion, cheese, and salt. Mix well.
2. Beat egg yolks and add. Stir in cooked macaroni.
3. Beat egg whites to form soft peaks. Fold into macaroni mixture.
4. Pour into a buttered casserole and sprinkle with paprika. Bake at 350° for 1 hour.

Macaroni Dried Beef Casserole

3 Tbsp. butter Makes 8 servings
2 Tbsp. onion, minced
1/4 cup mushrooms, chopped
3 Tbsp. flour
2 1/2 cups milk
1 cup uncooked macaroni
1 cup cheese, cubed
2 hard boiled eggs, chopped
1/4 lb. dried beef, chipped

1. Melt butter. Sauté onion and mushrooms until tender. Add flour and stir until smooth. Gradually add 1 cup of milk and stir until thickened. Remove from heat and stir in remaining milk.
2. Combine all other ingredients. Pour milk mixture over all. Mix well. Turn into greased casserole. Let stand 3-4 hours or overnight. Bake at 350° for 1 hour.

Dairyland Casserole

8 oz. noodles Makes 10-12 servings
1½ lb. ground beef
2 cups tomato sauce
⅛ tsp. worchestershire sauce
⅓ cup onion, chopped
1 Tbsp. green pepper, chopped
8 oz. cream cheese
1 cup cottage cheese
½ cup sour cream
3 Tbsp. melted butter

1. Cook noodles until tender. Drain and set aside.
2. Brown beef. Add tomato sauce, worchestershire sauce, onion, and pepper.
3. Combine cheeses and sour cream.
4. Butter large casserole. Pour in half of the noodles. Add cheese and cream mixture and cover with remaining noodles. Top with beef mixture. Drizzle melted butter over top. Bake at 350° for 30-45 minutes.